THE BOX

THE BOX
Answering the Faith of Unbelief

Craig Biehl

Carpenter's Son Publishing

Copyright © 2015 Craig Biehl

Published by Carpenter's Son Publishing
307 Verde Meadow Drive
Franklin, TN 37067

Unless otherwise indicated, Scripture quotations
are from the NEW AMERICAN STANDARD
BIBLE, © Copyright The Lockman Foundation
1960, 1962, 1963, 1968, 1971, 1972, 1973, 1975,
1977, 1988, 1995. Used by permission.

Cover Design: Christopher C. Pana
Text Design and Layout: Zoran Mandic

Library of Congress Control Number: 2014948657
ISBN: 978-1-942587-21-7

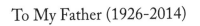

To My Father (1926-2014)

Where were you when I laid the
foundation of the earth?
—Job 38:4

TABLE OF CONTENTS

ANSWERING THE FAITH
OF THE ATHEIST

1

Quandary in a Garden
of Weeds

The clouds are alive with hues of red and orange. Butterflies flit about the flowering meadow as the sun disappears behind distant mountains. Without warning, Mr. C pushes me off the edge of a steep cliff towards the center of a boiling volcano. Cast into utter darkness, I scrape and tumble down the sharp lava slope and almost suffocate in a blizzard of goose feathers that once was my expensive, top-of-the-line, favorite parka. The inferno below dances in anticipation of my imminent arrival as I grab the branch of a huge Christmas tree jutting out from the side of the crater and hold on for dear life. As I dangle in the smoke, my neighbor Mr. C re-appears standing on the tree trunk, holding a red chain-saw. He looks at me with a devilish grin and pulls the ripcord. The buzz of the saw fades as I descend with the dismembered tree branch in my hands, a string of red and green lights wrapped around my neck, and some rather unseemly thoughts in my head about Mr. C! As I fall closer and closer to the abyss an Apache helicopter appears and peppers me with high-caliber bullets. "Hello?!" I yell in disgust. "Ever hear of a rescue mission?!" Nearing my certain doom, I cry out with weeping and gnashing of teeth for mercy when I hear a soft voice and feel a gentle hand on my shoulder. I begin to shake. Crying again for help, my desperate plea is answered by an epiphany, a celestial and rapturous voice: "Wake up dear."

*****

The morning sun glows warmly on the horizon as an exhausted Mr. A sits deep in thought on a pile of dirt in his garden. He had intended to pull weeds, but is bothered by the thoughts that kept him awake for most of the night. He chuckles at his nightmare and wonders how a few hot peppers before bedtime could produce such realistic and ridiculous drama. But that was just a sideshow. Something bigger is on Mr. A's mind—something real, beyond his mere earthly existence and the crazy world of jalapeño-inspired dreams.

What, then, is bothering Mr. A? Well, in the span of a few weeks he has gone from being a hard-core atheist to a rather non-committal agnostic, and he doesn't really know why. His recent conversations with his friendly neighbor Mr. C were unlike any he had experienced with other Christians over the years, and he is still not sure what to make of it all. Mr. C didn't fit the description of an arrogant and ignorant hypocrite, and that was a problem.

For the first time in his life, Mr. A is questioning his own ability to make claims about the existence of God. And worse, he is no longer sure where he would go when he died, a question made more urgent by his nighttime adventure, perhaps. In countless discussions with other religious folks (sometimes arguments, sometimes near riots), Mr. A had always walked away confident in his ability to tackle the big questions and convinced that he could accept or reject the arguments for God and Christianity as he saw fit. Today, however, he is not so sure. And so he sits, deep in thought on a pile of dirt in his garden as he ponders the delicate beauty of a butterfly on a nearby flower. Mr. C approaches...

Mr. C: Good morning Mr. A, are you in need of a lawn chair? Weeds do find it difficult to grow when they are being sat upon, but it may be a bit time consuming, I think. Should I bring you lunch later, oh troubler of dandelions?

Mr. A: You are too witty for me today, oh troubler of atheists. Pushed anybody into a volcano lately?

Mr. C: A what?

Mr. A: Never mind.

Mr. C: Okay [looking a bit perplexed]. Interesting you should use a biblical reference, Mr. A, is that possible?

Mr. A: I can still remember a Bible story about some nasty king calling a prophet the 'troubler of Israel.' My parents made us all go to Sunday school when we were little, thinking it might teach us a few things and keep us out of trouble.

Mr. C: Did it work?

Mr. A: I suppose that depends who you ask. It certainly did not keep me from pondering my existence on a pile of dirt in my garden.

Mr. C: No doubt the neighbors will think you have good reason to do so.

Mr. A: I intended to pull weeds, but I can't stop thinking about your illustration of the little brown box. I lost a great deal of sleep over it last night. How could something so simple say something so profound, and how did I miss it for all of these years?

Mr. C: I am glad that you have been thinking about it.

Mr. A: I am not about to join your Bible study, Mr. C, but the idea that my

views of God are built on faith,
and blind, unjustified faith at that,
is not comforting. Perhaps I might
visit your study group someday, but
don't hold your breath.

Mr. C: I will not hold my breath, Mr. A, but
I will continue to pray. In the
meantime, I do enjoy our talks, I hope
they can continue.

Mr. A: I would enjoy that, though my wife
might have something to say about it
—she is protective of my sleep, you
know. In any event, I do agree that
pulling the weeds would be more
effective than sitting on them, so I
best get on with it. But one more
thing, Mr. C—by any chance is your
chain saw red?

Mr. C: Why yes, Mr. A, how did you know it
was red? Would you like to borrow it?
Mr. A? Mr. A!? Why are you running
away?

Mr. A is thinking. And more than that, he
is considering what he thought impossible

just a few weeks earlier. He enjoys his talks with Mr. C, but they challenge him to the very core of his beliefs. Moreover, he was graciously able to answer the toughest questions Mr. A was able to throw at him. But why? What had Mr. C said that had brought Mr. A to his crisis of faith? And what was it about Mr. C's little brown box that cost Mr. A his sleep?

We'll soon go back in time to listen to the talks between Mr. A and Mr. C that brought Mr. A to his reflections in the garden. But before we do, we need to set the stage with some preliminary remarks about the nature of atheism, arguments, and unbelief in general.

2

Atheism Can Be a Bit Intimidating

A few years ago, I stumbled upon an article in the Wall Street Journal entitled, "Hitchens Book Debunking The Deity Is Surprise Hit."[1] Other titles, such as *The God Delusion, God is Not Great: How Religion Poisons Everything*, and *Letter to a Christian Nation* are wildly popular. "This is atheism's moment," declared one publisher. They are even "flying off the bookshelves" in the Bible Belt, said another (though suspicion has it that Christians are buying the books to study the tactics of their antagonists).[2] Debunking God is big business.

Atheists like to argue that science and

reason have delivered us from the unscientific and naive faith of religion. Modern folks no longer need an imaginary god for comfort or to explain the world. Reasonable people examine the facts of the universe, draw scientific conclusions, and leave the obsolete notion of a god on the bookshelf with other fairy tales.

Perhaps this sounds familiar? For the modern university student it may have been the morning lecture. Imagine happy young Christians prancing off to college to find everything they hold dear mocked and dismissed as foolish. "Do you seriously believe Jonah was in a whale for three days and lived, or that all people and animals descended from the passengers on Noah's ark? Can you reasonably and scientifically believe the earth was created in six days, or that the first woman was formed from the rib of the first man, and that the *universally accepted* theory of evolution is false?" And topping it all off (with a lowering of the voice, raising of an eyebrow, and peering over the eye glasses), "you don't *reeeally* take the Bible *literally*, do you?"

It can be a bit intimidating. Right or wrong, no one enjoys being viewed as an unscientific dunce. The pressure to modify biblical truth and history to make them acceptable to modern sensibilities is pervasive and strong, especially if one seeks the favor of the academic community or public opinion, to say nothing of the peer pressure that young students feel. We are daily tempted to lower God to our level, as one who is also subject to the "natural" laws of the universe, as opposed to the One who created, upholds, and transcends them.

In this short study, we will examine the "reasonable" and "scientific" claims of the atheist and agnostic as compared to the "unreasonable" and "blind" faith of the Christian. Could it be that the reverse is actually true? Could it be that Christian faith is neither blind nor unreasonable, while the best arguments of atheism and agnosticism are built on unsupportable leaps of blind faith?

The results may surprise you.

Endnotes

[1] Jeffrey A. Trachtenberg, June 22, 2007, p. B1.

[2] Ibid.

3

The Sweeping Claims of the Atheist

Concerning God, Man, and Everything in the Universe

Before we return to the friendly feud between the disturbers of dandelions and atheists, we need to first examine how far-reaching atheism's claims really are. At first glance, an atheist's claim that "God does not exist" appears to be little more than a simple statement about the existence of God. Yet it is much more.

First, to say that God does not exist implies many things about the nature of people and everything else in the universe, as well as God. For instance, to say God does not exist is to say that everything is uncreated, or is responsible for its own beginning, order, and ongoing existence. To say that God does not exist is to say the laws of physics and biology are not created, ordered, and sustained by God, but operate with precise order and set patterns ("laws") by themselves. To say that God does not exist is to say that all the love, thought, and physical existence of people exist by themselves, apart from God's wisdom and power. To say that God does not exist is to say that anything and everything has a beginning, existence, and purpose apart from God. However the atheist may attempt to explain the source, order, and magnificence of the universe—evolution or otherwise—it has nothing to do with "God." In an ultimate sense, everything came from nothing.

Thus, the claim that "God does not exist" is far more sweeping than appears at first sight, because it concerns the nature of everything that exists, has existed, or will ever exist. To say that God does not exist is to say what can and cannot be true of the ultimate origin, purpose, and meaning of everything. And while the atheist may humbly admit ignorance of many things in this world, this he knows for certain: The universe and everything in it is not created, ordered, and sustained by God, for God does not exist.

Concerning Knowledge, Truth, and Ultimate Authority

Second, in addition to sweeping assertions concerning the nature of God, mankind, and everything in the universe, similar claims are implied concerning the nature of knowledge, truth, and ultimate authority. As atheists claim to exist independently of God, so they believe they can observe, interpret, and make true statements about the nature of the universe apart from God. In other words, true knowledge, absolute truth, and ultimate authority to know and speak truth exist apart from God. God's explanation of the source and nature of reality is unnecessary, because everything can be observed and interpreted authoritatively from the limited perspective of people. And while the atheist may admit the possibility of holding false opinions, in denying God's existence he declares his own opinion or interpretation of reality as true and authoritative. In other words, to assert that all life exists without God creating and sustaining it is to presume one's own ability to accurately and authoritatively explain the ultimate origin, purpose, and meaning of life. Of course, few would dare call themselves the ultimate authority and determiner of truth, and their own interpretation of reality as absolute truth. Yet, atheists do exactly that.[1] When they deny God's existence and explanation of the universe, they presume their own limited vantage point to be the ultimate place of authority. And while atheists properly admit their ignorance concerning many things, they remain *certain* that God does not exist, that nothing of reality is created, ordered, or sustained by God, and that their limited vantage point is sufficient to make such authoritative statements of "truth."[2] Whether or not this assumption is reasonable will be examined later, but note well that the wide scope of the atheist's claims concerning God, man, and everything in the universe also applies to the nature of knowledge, truth, and ultimate authority. To assert one's own personal explanation of the source and ultimate nature of reality as true makes oneself the ultimate authority and determiner of truth. In this regard, atheists have assumed the place of the God they deny.

Concerning Morality

Third, it naturally follows that the ultimate judge of the nature of God, mankind, reality, knowledge, truth, and ultimate authority will be the ultimate judge of right and wrong. To assume no accountability to God is to assume human opinion is the highest moral authority, and the human will is free to do as it pleases (subject to *man-made* constraints). When people assume that God does not exist, they make their own rules.[3] This is not to say that all atheists live immoral lives relative to non-atheists, or that atheists do not have their own reasons for living a "moral" life.[4] It is just to say that a denial of God's existence is a claim of independence from God's law and judgment. "No God" infers no ultimate standard of right and wrong, no ultimate accountability, and no ultimate judgment. Thus, the claims of the atheist are comprehensive in their ethics, extending to the moral government of the universe, the ultimate destination of people after death, and whether or not people will be held accountable in the hereafter for bad behavior in the here and now. To say that God does not exist is to say a great deal.

Endnotes

[1] Even if the atheist should grant that his opinion is no more ultimately authoritative than another's opinion, assuming that God does not exist grants ultimate authority to one's own interpretation of reality, nonetheless.

[2] Of course, many today would deny that anyone can make authoritative statements of truth, though such a statement is itself a self-contradicting claim of truth. The contradiction is easily illustrated by the exaggerated statement, "There is no such thing as truth, and that's the truth!"

[3] Friedrich Nietzsche, a 19th Century German

philosopher and ardent opponent of Christianity, wrote that "a virtue needs to be our *own* invention, our *own* most personal need and self-defense: in any other sense, a virtue is just dangerous." "The most basic laws of preservation and growth require that everyone should invent his *own* virtues" [his emphasis]. Friedrich Nietzsche, *The Anti-Christ: A Curse on Christianity*, in *The Anti-Christ, Ecce Homo, Twilight of the Idols, and Other Writings*. Ed. Aaron Ridley and Judith Norman, trans. Judith Norman. Cambridge Texts in the History of Philosophy (Cambridge: Cambridge University Press, 2005), 9-10, §11. Consistent with the principles of the theory of evolution, Nietzsche's atheism led to the exaltation of power: "Good" is "everything that enhances people's feeling of power, will to power, power itself," while the "bad" is "everything stemming from weakness." "Happiness" is "the feeling that power is *growing*, that some resistance has been overcome. *Not* contentedness, but more power; *not* peace, but war; *not* virtue, but prowess… The weak and failures should perish: first principle of *our* love of humanity. And they should be helped to do this. What is more harmful than any vice? Active pity for all failures and weakness Christianity" (4, §2). "The Christian idea of God God as a god of the sick… is one of the most corrupt conceptions of God the world has ever seen" (15, §18).

[4] Nietzsche despised Christian morality, but not all atheists are as consistent with the moral implications of their view as Nietzsche. Many claim a basis for morality that closely reflects Christian morality, even while their worldview affirms evolutionary

natural selection and survival of the fittest. They presume the Christian worldview even as they deny it. The same is true of their practice of science, philosophy, or any other discipline. The truth of the Christian worldview is presumed when the universe is assumed to be ordered according to uniform and consistent laws, and not according to random and unpredictable chaos. An adequate discussion of this point is beyond the scope of this book. But note that the atheist does not and cannot live according to a consistent application of his own professed principles. Atheists necessarily live as if God exists, even while denying His existence.

4

Arguments Rest on Basic Assumptions

One more thing before we return to Mr. A and Mr. C's wrangling. Faithful Christians of every age are confronted with the unbelieving arguments of some of the greatest minds in history. Contemporary opponents of Christianity often have advanced degrees and may be experts in their field of study. For the average Christian trained in Sunday school, however, it can be a bit intimidating. Must the Christian earn a PhD to answer a PhD? Moreover, the number and variety of arguments for and against Christianity are boundless. How does the busy Christian begin to grasp the huge volume of material? The mere thought can be depressing. And while God needs no ultimate defense (His will and purpose *will be* accomplished), Christians have been commanded to participate in the privilege of declaring and defending the faith.[1] How, then, can believers adequately defend their faith in Christ in the face of such weighty and sophisticated opposition?

Fortunately, as varied and sophisticated as the arguments against the Christian faith may be, they are all built on the same assumptions. And like beautiful buildings, great arguments are only as good as their foundations. Therefore, if the starting assumptions of an argument against the existence of God are worthless, the conclusion will be worthless, regardless of the argument's sophistication. Interestingly, many false arguments against Christian truth or faith are quite logical when their conclusions logically follow their starting assumptions. To dispute such arguments without challenging the starting assumptions is futile. Leaving starting assumptions unchallenged when the conclusion follows those assumptions merely encourages unbelief by giving the impression that unbelieving arguments cannot be logically refuted. Any logical argument will be exposed as false if the starting assumptions are shown to be false. Therefore, if the faulty assumptions of the atheist can easily be identified and shown to be untrue, the ability to refute the most sophisticated arguments can be made available to all Christians.[2]

The nature of basic or foundational assumptions will be explained in the following chapters, but a few introductory remarks will help set the stage. Briefly, all people interpret what they see, hear, taste, touch, smell, and think about according to a standard of truth or authority. They trust (have faith) in this authority for the ultimate meaning of things. For instance, Christian and atheist scientists may agree on the observed laws of physics, yet one views them as the result of time and chance, and the other as the work of God. Though viewing the same facts, they trust in a different standard of truth or authority to interpret them. Scripture, as God's Word, is the ultimate authority and object of faith for the believing scientist, while the ultimate authority and object of faith for the atheist lies elsewhere (as we will soon see below).

In each case, the reasonableness and trustworthiness of one's ultimate authority or object of faith is at issue. Like a beautiful building on a faulty foundation, if the assumed authority on which atheists build their arguments is unreasonable and untrustworthy, so their arguments are also unreasonable and untrustworthy. This is true even if the logic of the argument is valid, with the conclusion rightly following the premise. Some of the soundest logical arguments are false because they are built on faulty premises or assumptions.

Endnotes

[1] The New Testament is replete with exhortations to preach, teach, and share the Gospel. With respect to defending the faith, Christians are to "contend earnestly for the faith" (Jude 3), and to "always" be "ready to make a defense to everyone who asks you to give an account for the hope that is in you" (1 Peter 3:15). In many cases, proclaiming and defending the Gospel are inseparable, as with Paul's defense in Acts 22. In one sense, to proclaim Christ and the Gospel as true involves defending why someone

should believe it versus something else. Defending the faith involves proclaiming it, and vice versa.

[2] Answering highly technical arguments built on those assumptions can be left to the experts. This is not to say that Christians need not study specific and detailed apologetic arguments in defense of the Christian faith, nor is it to put down the excellent work of Christian scientists and philosophers in their defense of Christianity. It is just to say that Christians need not have a PhD in philosophy to answer the basic philosophical objections to Christianity, or a PhD in biology or genetics to adequately answer the objections of their biology professor.

5

The Presumption of Omniscience

Identifying and demonstrating that the sophisticated arguments of atheism are built on unreasonable assumptions of faith involves asking the simple question, "How do you know what you claim to know?" Careful and gracious application of this question is the surest method for exposing atheism as unreasonable and unscientific. Of course, principles may be easy to learn, while their effective use in different situations may require time and experience (as with baseball, the violin, *and* apologetics). Nonetheless, as illustrated by the dialogue between our very own Mr. Christian ("C") and

Mr. Atheist ("A"),[1] this simple method is easy to learn and effective when used with wisdom and grace. Also, we will see that *atheists presume a measure of knowledge only possessed by the very God they deny.* Let's listen in...

Mr. C: Mr. A, great to see you. Are you well?

Mr. A: I am, thank you. And you?

Mr. C: I am well, thank you. Can I ask you a question, Mr. A?

Mr. A: Of course, Mr. C, but no doubt you will be at me again for my atheism.

Mr. C: You are my friend, Mr. A, and I would like that friendship to extend into eternity.

Mr. A: I do appreciate your attitude.

Mr. C: Here is my question. I have on my desk a beautiful antique box with a rustic brown finish. Can you tell me what is inside my little brown box, Mr. A?

Mr. A: Jewelry, perhaps?

Mr. C: I am afraid not. Do you have another guess?

Mr. A: I have not seen the box, and I have

not opened the box—how could I
know what is in the box?

Mr. C: Your answer is quite reasonable, Mr.
A. You most readily and humbly
admit your human limitations. How
about my garage, Mr. A, do you know
what is in my garage?

Mr. A: You know I have never been in your
garage. I have no idea what is in your
garage, though I know it does not
contain your cars.

Mr. C: It's a bit too crowded, I'm afraid. Tell
me, have you traveled through outer
space recently, or left your physical
body to roam around another
dimension?

Mr. A: Do I look like Dr. Who, Mr. C?

Mr. C: Do you agree, then, that you are
currently limited to three, maybe four
dimensions of existence?

Mr. A: Of course I am limited. I am also
limited according to my physical
abilities and in my ability to
understand your choice of questions,
Mr. C.

Mr. C: Do more than three dimensions exist? More than four, five, ten, or a hundred?

Mr. A: You tell me, Mr. C, how could I possibly know? I have never been beyond my earthly existence to render a guess. You are asking me questions that I cannot possibly answer. Do tell me your point, Mr. C.

Mr. C: Mr. A, does God exist?

Mr. A: Of course not, I am an atheist.

Mr. C: I know you are an atheist, and up until now you have been reasonable in admitting your human limitations. Why have you gone from being entirely reasonable to utterly irrational?

Mr. A: What do you mean, 'utterly irrational'? There is absolutely no evidence for the existence of God. You are the one claiming that someone we cannot see exists; perhaps the burden of proof is on you to prove to me that God exists.

Mr. C: I am unable to prove to your satisfaction that God exists.

Mr. A: That is exactly my point, Mr. C. There is no evidence for God, and you have admitted as much in saying you cannot prove to me He exists. I am surprised you have given up so soon.

Mr. C: I did not say there is no evidence for God, Mr. A. What I mean is I cannot, by argument alone, convince you *to your satisfaction* that God exists, as you are confronted with the evidence of His existence everywhere and at all times, yet still do not believe He exists. If the entire universe declares God's glory, including the design and order of all created existence, the provision of all good things, and your own conscience and consciousness,[2] how can I bring to you some new or additional proof that will convince you that He exists? In this way I cannot prove to you He exists, though the evidence for His existence is clear, conspicuous, comprehensive, and compelling, to such an extent that the Bible says you are without excuse for not believing in God and giving Him honor and thanks.[3]

Mr. A: I know, I know, that was last week's discussion. So, why the questions?

Mr. C: You are willing to admit your human limitations with respect to my brown box and garage, and your limited human existence. How, then, at the same time can you claim to know about everything in the universe?

Mr. A: Know everything in the universe!? I claimed no such thing, Mr. C. What have you been smoking? I know you were a hippie in the sixties, were you not, Mr. C?

Mr. C: Well, I… don't change the subject. But tell me, what would you have to know to tell me with certainty that God does not exist? Would you not have to know all that can be known of the entire universe *and beyond* before you can with certainty say that God does not exist?

Mr. A: I am not sure, I have never thought of it that way.

Mr. C: In order for one to say that God does not exist with certainty, one would have to know all that could be known about everything in the universe *and beyond*, including every possible dimension. In saying God does not exist, you are implying that you are omniscient and have sufficient data and ability to know with certainty that God does not exist.

Mr. A: I am doing no such thing.

Mr. C: I know you would never overtly claim to have infinite knowledge, an attribute of God. Nonetheless, one would still need to possess knowledge about everything in the universe *and beyond* to say God does not exist—an attribute of the very God that atheists say does not exist. And while you have been most reasonable in admitting that you cannot possibly know what is in my wooden box and garage without actually looking inside them, you are at the same time willing to make a claim that requires a knowledge and ability infinitely greater than what is required to know the contents of my wooden box and garage. You seem to have gone from a very rational position, admitting your human limitations with respect to the universe, to a very irrational one that speaks as if you know all things, which you admit you do not.

Mr. A: I look at the universe and I do not see the evidence for God, so there is no God.

Mr. C: Are you telling me that what you cannot see cannot exist? Is that not taking the place of God by saying, in effect, that what you cannot see or know cannot exist? Are you saying that what can and cannot exist in the universe is determined by your limited understanding of it? Is that reasonable?

Mr. A: I know that you just want me to go to heaven, but my human limitations require me to eat.

Mr. C: So God has created us, Mr. A. I look

forward to our next conversation.

Mr. A: I look forward to it as well, Mr. C.

This simple illustration reveals the basic flaw of the atheist's claim. On the one hand, Mr. A is reasonable to concede the limits of his knowledge in admitting his ignorance of the content of Mr. C's wooden box and garage. On the other hand, he is unreasonable in claiming that God does not exist, for he would need to know everything about the entire universe and beyond to legitimately make such a claim. He would have to be God to deny God, whom he says does not exist. And while he acknowledges his limited ability to know many aspects of the universe (including the box and garage), he knows for sure it is all uncreated, self-existing, self-ordering, and unrelated to God, for God does not exist.[4] The assumed ability to make "authoritative" assertions about that which cannot possibly be known apart from omniscience or a direct revelation from God is basic to all atheistic arguments. This is the foundation or assumption of faith upon which atheistic arguments are built. In short, the atheist has faith in his or her own ability to know what cannot possibly be known apart from omniscience or a direct revelation from God. The atheist presumes the ultimate authority or standard of truth to be his or her own opinion. At issue, then, is whether or not this is a trustworthy and reasonable foundation for the atheists' arguments. As we have seen, if the foundation is faulty, so are the conclusions of the argument. The following discussion of miracles will further illustrate this principle.

Endnotes

[1] The technique of using illustrative dialogues was often used by Cornelius Van Til in his writings. Though the sophistication and insight of dialogues written by Van Til far exceed those I have written, I have nonetheless borrowed his technique.

[2] See Psalm 19:1-6, Acts 14:17, Romans 1:19-21, 2:14-15. Theologians call this "general" revelation as distinguished from "special" revelation, Scripture.

[3] All people have a "sense of divinity," a knowledge of God. Romans 1:18-21 tells us that all people "know" God because God has made Himself known to them, though unbelievers sinfully suppress this knowledge. Believers know God in a different way

than unbelievers, as their knowledge includes a true understanding and love for God, whereas unbelievers suppress and distort the knowledge of God in order to deny Him. When Scripture speaks of unbelievers not knowing God, it refers to the intimate and personal knowledge of God possessed by believers.

[4] Indeed, no argument or evidence could be presented to convince him otherwise apart from the power and work of the Holy Spirit and Scripture. The Bible clearly teaches that unbelievers are "hostile" to God (Colossians 1:21, Romans 8:7), they "cannot understand" and "cannot accept the things of the Spirit of God" (1 Corinthians 2:14), they are "darkened in their understanding" (Ephesians 4:18), and spiritually "dead" such that the excellent things of God and Christ are viewed as "foolish" (Ephesians 2:1, 1 Corinthians 1:18-23). Everywhere they are confronted with the evidence and knowledge of God in their hearts and in the beauty and blessings of the created universe, yet they "suppress the truth" of God "in unrighteousness" (Romans 1:18-22). Accordingly, unbelievers are neither objective nor neutral in their understanding and interpretation of God and His created universe.

6

Are Miracles Reasonable?

Atheists typically deny the reality of the miracles and extraordinary events in Scripture. Their arguments have been influential in academic circles, where scholars offer alternative explanations of biblical events long held to be literal and historical. Some atheists label the biblical accounts of miracles as allegory or myth, even though Christ considered them historical. Particularly embarrassing to some are descriptions of Jonah in the belly of a fish, and Noah saving the animal kingdom and human race in an ark. Such "children's stories" are little better than fairy tales to many.

But how are we to view these accounts? Can a Christian in the modern world reasonably hold these events to be historical in the face of harsh criticism and intellectual disdain? Let's return to the ongoing discussion between Mr. A and Mr. C to show that believers should never be intimidated by arguments against the truth of miracles and extraordinary events recorded in Scripture. We will see that atheists arguing against the reality of biblical miracles operate on the same unreasonable assumption of omniscience illustrated above.

Mr. A: Mr. C, have you been well?

Mr. C: Yes, thank you Mr. A, and you?

Mr. A: I am well, thank you. I have been doing some reading; could I ask you a few questions?

Mr. C: Please do, Mr. A. I am interested in what you have discovered.

Mr. A: Do you believe the Bible is true?

Mr. C: Yes, of course.

Mr. A: Do you believe that Jonah was actually in the belly of a fish for three days, was spit up onto a beach, and took to preaching in good health?

Mr. C: Yes, of course.

Mr. A: [Smiling] Very funny, Mr. C.

Mr. C: I actually believe the event took place exactly as written.

Mr. A: My dear Mr. C, surely you jest. Might I also propose that reindeer fly and the Easter bunny delivers baskets of candy? I can hardly, I can't, I'm...

Mr. C: Do you need to sit down, Mr. A? Not only do I believe it, it is most reasonable that Jonah could be in the belly of a fish for three days on his way to a preaching assignment. Indeed, all of the miracles of the Bible are most reasonable and logical.

Mr. A: 'Reasonable and logical,' Mr. C? I can understand that, contrary to reason, you must believe it on faith—but how can you possibly say that all miracles are 'logical'? [With a lowering of his voice, raising of an eyebrow, and peering over his eye glasses]: You don't *reeeally* take the Bible *literally*, do you, Mr. C?

Mr. C: You sound like my daughter's college professor. Well, first, I do not believe miracles should be accepted according to faith that is contrary to reason or evidence. True faith is reasonable and justified. It all depends on your starting point. As God has infinite power and created all things, including all laws, He is above all laws of 'nature' and is not subject to their limitations. It is therefore reasonable that a God of such power and control over the entire universe could have Jonah in the belly of a fish for three days, or three hundred years, if He so desired. So it is that Christ can walk on water, raise the dead, and so on.

Mr. A: So, do you believe that Noah really built an ark, and that all of the existing species of life are derived from the inhabitants of the ark? And how do you think Noah and his family were able to feed them and clean up the consequences of so many animals? Did he have an additional ark or two to carry enough food to feed such a zoo? This is so beyond the pale that I cannot believe I am discussing it.

Mr. C: You forgot the additional problem of how he managed to gather two of every kind of living creatures and have them freely and in good order enter into the ark to take their place in their respective stalls. 'Excuse me, Mr. Lion? Could you get your mate and board the ark at 0800 hours? And don't worry, we'll have plenty of fresh meat for you to eat, so stay away from the unicorns!' 'Oh dear, the armadillos are late, and where are the elephants?' There are more difficulties than you have stated, Mr. A.

Mr. A: And you still believe it is reasonable and logical to believe it?

Mr. C: Yes.

Mr. A: Are you serious? Do you really, I mean, how can you, I... I...

Mr. C: I really wish you would sit down, Mr.

A. I do know CPR but I might think twice about the mouth-to-mouth part. Of course, you would no longer be an atheist...

Mr. A: Too funny, Mr. C. Do explain your point.

Mr. C: Alright. Just as with Jonah, a God of infinite power who created and upholds all things can do all things. The ark is child's play for God. Our problem with the account of the ark is we try to explain it according to 'natural' principles, according to our own limitations, without God. Noah built the ark, but it took the infinite power of God to fill it, maintain it, and populate the earth with animals. The God who can speak and make a universe from nothing can certainly work with Noah to gather and preserve the animals.

Mr. A: Do you also believe that Christ was born of a virgin?

Mr. C: Absolutely. Scripture clearly teaches that God the Son took upon Himself human flesh to act as our substitute, to pay the penalty for our sin in our place.[1] As God created and upholds all things, including procreation, He is not subject to their limitations. As with all miracles, God is not subject to the constraints of the physical laws he created and upholds. Nothing is impossible with God.

Mr. A: But God does not exist, Mr. C, so such miracles do not exist.

Mr. C: Then we are back to square one with our original conversation. In order for you to prove to me that miracles do not exist, you must prove to me that God does not exist. And, as we have discussed, that would require you to know everything about every aspect of the universe and beyond. The same omniscience required for you to deny God's existence is required for you to deny miracles.

Mr. A: Okay, then why do some who call themselves Christians admit that the story of Jonah, Noah and the ark, or the flood are not historical facts, but merely stories used to make a theological point?

Mr. C: Good question. If their starting point in interpreting Scripture was the person and nature of God as He has revealed Himself to be in Scripture, they would not resort to such things. Perhaps they need to learn some proper theology and apologetics, Mr. A.

Mr. A: Well, I must say they are not helpful to your cause, for they do seem to validate my own views. You would think that if they believed God to be the source of all things and as powerful and in control of the universe as you believe, they would know they are in no place to question what God could or could not do, and would have no problem with Jonah in a fish or Noah and the ark as history.

Mr. C: I confess, Mr. A, you are quite correct.

Mr. A: Anyway, I am thankful for them, for they do encourage my unbelief.

Mr. C: Perhaps you could speak with them and convince them to be a bit more consistent with the theology they claim to embrace.

Mr. A: No thanks, Mr. C, that's your job. We'll talk again!

In the second encounter of our friendly neighbors, we see the principle established in their first encounter at work again, though it may not be as obvious. We see that Mr. A's rejection of miracles is based on his denial of the existence of God. Since God does not exist, there can be no miracles. Of course, this ignores the problem of defining miracles in a universe where no God upholds the "laws of nature," for what then prevents a "law" from changing from one day to the next in a world founded on random chance?[2] But I digress.

For Mr. C, miracles are both reasonable and logical. An infinitely powerful God is not constrained by the laws He created and upholds. Miracles are merely God exerting His power in a different way than he upholds the laws of the universe He created and sustains. Both the uniform laws of "nature," and the miracles that are contrary to those laws, equally require the infinite power of God to exist. Thus, one's view of God determines one's view of miracles and the extraordinary events of Scripture. To deny the possibility of miracles, one must first prove that God does not exist. And, as we noted earlier, one would need to know everything about everything in the universe *and beyond* to legitimately deny the existence of God. Those who cannot know the contents of Mr. C's antique box or garage without looking inside them cannot possess such knowledge. Moreover, in light of God as the source of all things and determiner of what is possible in the universe, it is unfortunate that some who profess to know Him would presume to know what God did and did not do in history, contrary to God's clear testimony in Scripture.[3] In making such claims, the professing believer acts according to the principles of the atheist, and assists the unbeliever in justifying *unbelief.*

So we see, as with the first illustration, that the ultimate problem with atheism is the unwarranted and irrational assumptions upon which it rests. And with respect to miracles, until one can prove that God does not exist, one cannot prove that Jonah could not be in the belly of a fish for three days, or that lions and tigers and bears (oh my!) could not accompany Noah on an extended cruise on an ark. God can speak and make a universe, so what's the problem with Jonah in a fish and Noah and the ark?

Endnotes

[1] Scripture not only teaches the virgin birth as something accomplished by God's infinite power, but also its theological necessity. Christ could not be our sinless savior if He was subject to original sin as a physical descendent of Adam through a human father. Moreover, given the curse upon Jeconiah of the royal Davidic line (Jeremiah 22:30), no physical descendent of Jeconiah could sit on David's throne. Joseph, Christ's earthly father, was a direct descendent of the royal line through Jeconiah (see Matthew 1:1-17), so Christ was of the royal line. But Christ was not subject to the curse upon Jeconiah's "seed" or physical descendents because He was born of a virgin. He was not a physical descendent of Jeconiah. Moreover, by virtue of the curse upon Jeconiah's descendents, Christ is the only person who could possibly sit on the Davidic throne in fulfillment of the Davidic covenant. The virgin birth, therefore, is an absolute theological necessity and a marvelous picture of God's providence.

[2] Apart from God, no rational basis for the uniformity or existence of the "laws of nature" is possible, as all existence and events would be according to random chance. Nevertheless, most atheists assume the Christian view of an ordered universe in all areas of life, including science. But the only basis for that ordered universe is the God they deny. And they also reject the miracles of Scripture, divinely prescribed departures from that order, thus affirming the Christian worldview they attempt to deny.

[3] No one acts entirely consistent with his or her espoused principles. Indeed, every time we sin we deny our professed affirmation of the Lordship of Christ. When professing believers affirm God alone is uncreated and eternal, the source of all things, they should not attempt to explain His works in history in a manner acceptable to the principles of those who deny that God is the ground of all of reality. This would be to deny the very God they profess. In this, they either fail to apply their stated principles or they have an improper view of God and act according to their improper view. The proper attitude for approaching Scripture is found in Isaiah 66:2: "'For My hand made all these things, thus all these things came into being,' declares the Lord. 'But to this one I will look, to him who is humble and contrite of spirit, and who trembles at My word.'"

7

The Problem of Evil and the Trinity

What about those arguments that profess to show contradictions in the content of Scripture, the foundation of the Christian faith? As we will soon see, this type of argument rests upon the same faith assumptions underlying the atheist's claim that God does not exist, and that the miracles of Scripture are not true. Let's listen as Mr. A and Mr. C discuss what is known as "the problem of evil."

Mr. A: Mr. C, seen any miracles lately?

Mr. C: You are still breathing, are you not, Mr. A?

Mr. A: [Laughing] Natural processes, Mr. C, natural processes. I have been doing some reading. Could I ask you a few questions?

Mr. C: Please do, I am interested in what you have discovered.

Mr. A: The Bible teaches that God is infinitely good, and will do what is good in every situation, is that correct?

Mr. C: Yes, that is true.

Mr. A: And the Bible says that God is all powerful and can do anything He wills?

Mr. C: Yes, that is also true.

Mr. A: Then your God cannot exist, for if God were all-powerful he could prevent evil, and if he were perfectly good he would certainly prevent evil. Given that evil exists, God is either less than perfectly good or less than infinitely powerful. Therefore, God as the Bible describes him cannot exist.

Mr. C: Mr. A, you have stated quite well what is sometimes called 'the problem

of evil.' I commend you on your
research.[1]

Mr. A: Then you will join my atheism club
this evening?

Mr. C: Thank you, perhaps not. Could I ask a
few questions before you go?

Mr. A: Absolutely.

Mr. C: The way you have stated the problem
of evil does pose a difficulty.

Mr. A: Yes, it is a logically valid argument, as
the conclusion follows from the
premise.

Mr. C: The conclusion appears to follow from
the premise as stated, but that does
not make the conclusion true, as the
premise might not be true. For
instance, how do we know a good
God will necessarily and always
prevent evil? Do good parents always
prevent every bad thing a child might
do, for reasons not understood by the
child?

Mr. A: Sure, but we are talking about God
here.

Mr. C: Yes, and God's ways are infinitely

above our ways. Your premise
excludes the possibility that God may
have allowed evil for reasons beyond
our understanding. Isaiah 55:8-9 says,
"'For My thoughts are not your
thoughts, neither are your ways My
ways,' declares the Lord. 'For as the
heavens are higher than the earth, so
are My ways higher than your ways,
and My thoughts than your
thoughts.'" Now, if God and His ways
are infinitely higher than us and our
ways, is it not reasonable that He
would know things we do not know
or could not know as finite human
beings?

Mr. A: Sure.

Mr. C: Is it fair to say that you deny God's
existence because you cannot
understand how evil can exist in a
world created by an infinitely good
and omnipotent God?

Mr. A: Correct.

Mr. C: I confess that I do not fully
understand the origin of evil in the

world, though the Bible teaches that it had its beginning in the will of a created angel. Many explanations for its origin seem inadequate, or appear to make God dependent on evil to accomplish His purposes, which is contrary to what Scripture says concerning His holy character. But, as with miracles, given that God is infinite and I am finite, I necessarily will not understand everything about God and His world. I can only know what He has chosen to reveal to me.

Mr. A: Isn't that a copout, Mr. C?

Mr. C: No, it is merely an acceptance of my limitations and dependence on God for all things, including His explanation of Himself and His universe. It is reasonable that we should be content not having answers to all of life's questions or solutions to things we cannot reconcile in our mind. If I could unravel all mysteries, I would be God. We do well to remember God's rebuke of Job,

'Where were you when I laid the foundations of the earth?'[2]

Mr. A: Well, that does not satisfy me. We may not have all the answers, but if we keep looking, we ultimately will.[3] In the present case, if I cannot reconcile God's character with the existence of evil in the world, then God does not exist.

Mr. C: It appears we are back to square one, Mr. A. Are you saying that if you cannot reconcile in your limited mind something God has revealed about Himself in Scripture, it cannot be true?

Mr. A: Yes.

Mr. C: So your understanding is the ultimate standard of what is true or what can or cannot exist? Could a reason exist that is beyond our present capacity to understand, one that God knows, that was not included in how you set up the problem of evil? Is every possibility in the universe exhausted by the way you stated the problem of evil? Could God know something we do not?

Mr. A: If He exists and is infinite, then He would know more than we do, and we would not have all the answers.

Mr. C: You previously admitted the limitations of your knowledge in not knowing what is in my antique box or garage, only to subsequently speak as if you knew everything about every aspect of the universe by denying God's existence. And now, though you remain limited in knowledge, you have denied the possibility of mystery with respect to evil, and have made your own understanding the ultimate judge of what can be true.[4] You have again assumed the place of God, in whom alone are all the answers to the mysteries of the universe. Mr. A, the Bible tells us that this was mankind's first sin—the attempt to take the place of God.

Mr. A: Okay, Mr. C, what then is the answer to the problem of evil?

Mr. C: Only God knows the answer, ultimately. But I do know this: He has revealed His character in the person of Christ, in His infinite love for sinners in bearing the infinite penalty of our sin upon Himself on the cross at Calvary, in His infinite hatred of sin, in requiring its penalty to be paid that we might be freed from its condemnation. We do know that moral evil had its beginning in the free will of the creature, and that it does not exist apart from the will of the creature. We know the world is cursed because of evil and that all suffering, in an ultimate sense, can be traced back to sin and its consequences. We do know that God has provided an infinite solution to evil, and that He provided it at infinite expense and suffering to Himself.

Mr. A: So many people seem to suffer for someone else's evil. It is painful to experience and painful to watch, while some of the answers appear simplistic or superficial to me.

Mr. C: The pain and difficulties of this life are profound, and I would be thoughtless in my own comfort to treat them superficially or callously. But despite the depth of the problem, I can take great comfort in God's perfect character as revealed in Christ, in His promise that righteousness will ultimately prevail and perfect justice will be done, that all unjust suffering will be more than fully recompensed, and all evil sufficiently punished.

Mr. A: Even though I do not believe in God, I must admit that I do hope there will be ultimate justice for the likes of Hitler, Stalin, and Mao. But I still find your explanation less than satisfying.

Mr. C: Yes, much remains a mystery, but we dare not presume to take the place of God in claiming to have all the answers. Regardless of the difficulties involved, we cannot deny our human limitations. We can, however, accept our place as God's creation and trust in Him who has all the answers. God alone runs the universe, and we should be happy to leave this responsibility to Him. Perhaps He will explain the ultimate origin of evil to me when I see Him in heaven. He has clearly revealed His goodness and omnipotence to us in the person and work of Christ. At the same time, for reasons beyond our present comprehension, He has allowed evil to exist. I do know that the way God deals with evil shows the excellence of His character, and being holy, He does not do moral evil that good may result. I also know freedom does not require the existence of evil, as we will be most free in heaven, where evil will not be an option. So, we are back where we started.[5]

Mr. A: Let me know when you get an answer.

Mr. C: My hope is that we will be able to ask Him together.

Mr. A: Oh no, here it comes. Dinner is
calling. We'll talk again.
Mr. C: I am looking forward to it.

To recap, the "problem of evil" as formulated by Mr. A is certainly a difficult question for the Christian. Indeed, Scripture confronts our limited understanding with many difficult questions, such as the nature of the Trinity (as will be discussed below), or God's predetermination of the events of the universe and the responsibility of man for his actions.

Here, as with all such difficult questions, limited human understanding cannot be the final judge of what can or cannot be true. The creation of the universe out of nothing, the person of Christ as 100 percent God and 100 percent man, the Trinity—these are divine mysteries that no logic can explain (though they are logical, given God's infinite and transcendent greatness as revealed in Scripture). The finite, created human being does not have infinite and exhaustive knowledge of God and His universe. Most important, our understanding does not constitute the final determiner of truth. So is the problem of evil really a problem? Yes and no. The suffering of this life reaches into the depths of our soul and challenges us in a profound way. Yet, we have great comfort in the perfect character of God as displayed in the person and saving work of Christ in defeating death and evil, and in God's ultimate righteous reign and rule over the universe in making all things right. And if Scripture is clear about anything, it is clear that God is infinitely good and infinitely powerful, and that His ways are infinitely above our ways. If the problem of evil demonstrates anything, it demonstrates that we are not God—a difficult truth for sinful humanity to embrace. To say God does not exist because I cannot understand the problem of evil is to make my limited understanding the final authority of what is true or what can or cannot exist. To do so is to take the place of God Himself, the first sin of Scripture and the heart of every sin since. The atheist may choose to repeat Lucifer's error, but the Christian need not be intimidated by it, for it is merely the validation of what Scripture says about the nature of sin and fallen mankind.

We turn now to a brief look at the doctrine of the Triune nature of God, another difficult question used by atheists to deny the existence of God.

Mr. A: Mr. C, is God three or one?

Mr. C: Both.

Mr. A: If I understand the Christian view correctly, it is wrong to believe in three Gods, but it is also wrong to believe in one God who merely manifests Himself three different ways at different times.

Mr. C: That is correct.

Mr. A: So, is refuting the existence of your God as simple as knowing basic arithmetic?

Mr. C: To some it would seem so, but that is far too simplistic. Scripture teaches that God is one personal being who eternally exists as three persons. Yet, He is not three Gods, but one.

Mr. A: Gee, that clears things up. How can I possibly accept something that sounds so irrational?

Mr. C: Remember, what appears to be irrational to you, given your limitations, is not irrational in God. God is perfect. He is not subject to the laws He created to order the universe, He transcends them.

Mr. A: So we come to another copout: Just claim God is too high, and the argument is over.

Mr. C: Are you saying because you cannot understand how God can be both three and one, He cannot exist? Or that because you cannot grasp or understand something, it cannot be true? Is your limited understanding really the ultimate determiner of truth?

Mr. A: I cannot see how God can be one and three persons at the same time. The Nicene and Athanasian Creeds appear to be complete nonsense to me.

Mr. C: God as a Trinity is indeed a mystery to us, but not to God, as He is not constrained by our understanding or the created limitations of the universe.

As He is infinitely higher than us, we cannot know Him unless He condescends to reveal Himself to us, and He has revealed Himself to us in Scripture as one personal God, eternally subsisting as three persons: God the Father, God the Son, and God the Holy Spirit.

Mr. A: Are you asking me to forsake reason?

Mr. C: No, only to admit your limitations as a finite, created being, who cannot exhaust the knowledge of our infinite God. The Trinity is God, and if we could fully understand Him, He would not be much of a God. Unfortunately, many who claim to be Christians agree with your approach, rejecting doctrines because they cannot fully understand or explain them.

Mr. A: I must admit that they do help my cause.

Mr. C: And please understand, I am not denying the use of logic or reason. God gave us minds, and He gave us logic to order our thinking. But He never gave them to us to deny His transcendence. This would be an irreverent use of logic, one that does not acknowledge God as infinitely greater than we are. We must submit to the authority of God in what He has told us about Himself. As much as we dislike admitting our weaknesses and limitations, we need to learn how to think in a manner that fully honors God and His infinite supremacy over us.

Mr. A: Interestingly, a Christian once told me that the law of non-contradiction is the final determiner of truth. This convinced me further that I could explain God away, since the Trinity is clearly a concept that appears to violate that law.

Mr. C: It is a helpful and valid law of logic, but it must bow to God's transcendence. Truth is what God says it is, and we know God by what He has chosen to reveal to us.

Mr. A: I must admit, when my arguments
concerning miracles or apparent
contradictions in Scripture are viewed
according to the infinite greatness of
God as revealed in Scripture, it does
take the wind out of my sails. I still
have a hard time accepting the idea
that I take the place of God in my
argumentation, but I will give it more
thought.

As with the "problem of evil," the Trinity
as revealed in Scripture is ultimately a mystery
beyond the limits of human understanding. In the
Trinity, we meet the God that is infinitely above
and beyond all things (and yet has condescended
to clearly and personally reveal Himself in time
and space to His creatures). To say that God
cannot exist as He has revealed Himself to exist
is to say He cannot be beyond what we can
understand, or above what we know to be the
laws of the universe. But on what authority can
one limit God? Is our finite understanding that
which determines what can or cannot exist? Is
our limited perspective the ultimate determiner

of truth? In this, the atheist is again operating on unwarranted faith in his or her ability to know what cannot possibly be known apart from revelation from God. In refusing to accept God's testimony about Himself, atheists make dogmatic statements about the ultimate nature of God and the universe, when they do not even know what is in their neighbor's antique box or garage. They declare what God can or cannot be from the vantage point of five senses, three dimensions, and seventy or so years on the earth, when knowledge of every aspect of the universe and beyond is required to justify their claim. God alone possesses such knowledge, and He alone can reveal to us with authority what He is like.

Endnotes

[1] Note that the "problem of evil" goes beyond the existence of calamities in the world that are directly or indirectly the result of God's judgments against moral sin, including the curse on the world in Genesis 3.

[2] Job 38:4. Job 38-42 is a most valuable passage for developing a proper humility in approaching God and His explanation of history and reality in light of our limitations.

[3] The Christian perspective is that we can never have infinitely exhaustive knowledge of God and the universe, even in heaven, as we are not and never will be God. It is only because Mr. A. denies God's existence, and cannot conceive of the vast difference between the God of the Bible and His creatures, that he contends mankind will some day have all the answers.

[4] Notice how the atheist is both reasonable and unreasonable at the same time. He is reasonable in admitting his limitations, but unreasonable in presuming to know what he cannot possibly know. He admits and denies his limitations at the same time. This is characteristic of all unbelief. People live as created beings in a universe created, upheld, and ordered by God, encompassed by the knowledge of God everywhere, even in their own hearts. Nevertheless, they presume a knowledge that they could not possibly possess, denying the reality that surrounds them and the truth that confronts them at every turn. They do this in all of life, denying God while assuming and living according to a reality that can only have its existence by the infinitely wise, creating, upholding, and ordering of the universe by the God of the Bible they deny.

[5] An adequate treatment of the various attempts to
     solve the problem of evil is beyond the scope of this
     short booklet. For a concise presentation and critique
     of proposed solutions to the problem of evil, see John
     M. Frame, *Apologetics to the Glory of God*
     (Phillipsburg, NJ: P&R Publishing, 1994), 149-190.

8

Miscellaneous Arguments

Though we have viewed a few short examples, the simple technique of asking, "How do you know what you claim to know?" can be used with any atheistic argument. For instance, some argue that God cannot act in time and space unless He is confined and constrained by time and space, contrary to Scripture's teaching that God transcends time and space and also acts within them. How can the limited perspective of the unbeliever, who himself is limited by time and space, conclude that the infinite God of the universe is so limited? As for logical, mathematical, or otherwise "scientific" arguments denying God's existence, God created, upholds, and transcends all things. He is not limited by the "natural" laws He created and sustains. Again, how could we possibly know that God is so limited unless He condescends to tell us? To the contrary, He has told us that He is infinitely beyond our understanding, though we can know what he has chosen to reveal to us about Himself. Nonetheless, many make unjustified statements about God based on faith in their own limited understanding, despite the fact that they cannot possibly know such things apart from God's revelation.

Others point to evil perpetrated in the world "in the name of God" as proof that God does not exist, for how could God be as good as Scripture describes Him if His creatures are so evil? Apart from the fact that Scripture tells us that sinful man will use God's name to commit evil, and that narrow is the way to salvation and few will enter therein, such pronouncements presume knowledge of the heart of every person in every age, and make the grand assumption that God has not been at work in any of them.

It is safe to say He is not at work in the hearts of those denying His existence, but beyond the obvious cases, Scripture tells us it is difficult to tell the wheat from the tares (the true from false believers). Understanding the heart of one person is difficult enough, let alone the heart of everyone that has ever existed.[1] Here again, the irrational presumption of omniscience underlying many atheistic arguments is at work.

And just for fun, perhaps you have heard the question, "if God were all powerful, could He make a rock so heavy He could not lift it?" Some pose this clever riddle, though not always seriously, to argue that God cannot possess boundless power. If God could make a rock so heavy that He could not lift it, He lacks boundless power because a rock could exist that God cannot lift. On the other hand, if God cannot make such a rock, He is again limited because He cannot make such a large rock. The simple answer is God can make a rock of infinite weight and He can lift it. He cannot be defined out of existence by clever riddles.

Endnotes

[1] Here again, God's rebuke of Job is instructive: "Will you really annul my judgment? Will you condemn Me that you may be justified?" (Job 40:8).

9

Summary

In our brief treatment of the unreasonable blind faith of the atheist, we observed that the assertion "God does not exist" is a sweeping claim concerning the ultimate nature of man, reality, knowledge, truth, authority, and ethics. In understanding the comprehensive scope of the claim, we are confronted with how ill-equipped the atheist is to make it. Moreover, we saw that the denial of God's existence is founded upon the atheist's unreasonable faith in his or her own opinion, and an implied assumption of knowing everything about everything in the universe and beyond.

We have also seen that miracles are reasonable and to be expected, given God's infinite power and control over the laws He created and upholds. To deny miracles, one must first prove God does not exist, since a person's view of God determines his or her view of miracles. Also, to deny God's existence because we cannot reconcile God's power and goodness with the existence of evil reduces God to that which we can fully understand. In so doing, we make our understanding the ultimate judge of what God can and cannot be, and take the place of God as the ultimate authority and determiner of truth. The same applies to arguments against the possibility of God being a Trinity.

These few examples reveal the false assumptions that underlie all arguments against the existence of God. In examining atheists' authority to make assertions about the ultimate nature of God and the universe, we asked the question, "How do you know what you claim to know?" We observed that all atheistic arguments rest upon unreasonable faith in human opinion. Any person limited to five senses, three or four dimensions, seventy or so years on earth, and unable to know even the contents of his neighbor's brown box and garage, cannot make trustworthy statements about the ultimate nature of God and the universe, apart from revelation from the God he claims does not exist. This is a problem for the atheist. For good reason Scripture tells us, "The fool has said in his heart, 'there is no God'" (Psalm 53:1).

We turn now to agnosticism. Having observed that a finite human being is incapable of making true statements about the ultimate nature of a transcendent God and His universe (apart from God's revelation), wouldn't agnosticism be a reasonable alternative given its claims of ignorance? Does our critique of atheism affirm agnosticism? Let's see...

ANSWERING THE FAITH
OF THE AGNOSTIC

10

The Sweeping Claims of the Agnostic

Concerning God, Man, and All Reality

Agnosticism varies from the more dogmatic claim that "the existence of God *cannot be known*," to the "kinder and gentler" version that alleges a *lack of evidence* to either affirm or deny that God exists. At first glance, these claims appear to humbly accept the limitations of human knowledge. On closer inspection, however, they say a great deal about God and the entire universe. For instance, they say that God does not exist, or if He does, He is either unable to make Himself known or has chosen not to make Himself known. Either possibility asserts something about the nature or intentions of the God that agnostics say cannot be known (more about this later).

Also, claims that God's existence cannot be known or that the evidence is lacking imply that nothing in the known universe bears the clear marks of divine origin—not Christ, Scripture, consciousness, conscience, reason, love, or the laws of physics and biology. They also imply that all the "miraculous"[1] beauty and design in the universe give no evidence of the greater wisdom of a designer. Therefore, the intended or unintended claims of agnostics are far more comprehensive than they first appear. Their claims concern the nature of everything that exists or has ever existed, and assert what can or cannot be true concerning ultimate reality. And while agnostics admit ignorance of many things, they claim to know for sure that nothing in the known universe gives evidence of the nature or existence of God.

Concerning Knowledge, Truth, and Ultimate Authority

In addition to sweeping assertions concerning the nature of God, mankind, and reality, agnostics imply similar claims with respect to the nature of knowledge, truth, and ultimate authority. As agnostics claim to exist independently of God, or at least claim that God is not necessary for their existence and knowledge, they believe they can observe, interpret, and make true statements about the ultimate nature of the universe apart from God's explanation of it. In other words, one can possess true knowledge, absolute truth, and ultimate authority to know and speak the truth without any dependence on God.

Like the atheist, the agnostic denies the need for God's explanation of the source and nature of reality. Despite considerable human limitations, he presumes his own ability to know and explain the ultimate nature of the universe. Thus, in declaring the existence and nature of God as unknowable, and therefore unnecessary for a proper explanation of reality, agnostics declare their own opinion or interpretation of reality as true and ultimately authoritative. Few would be so brash as to declare their own interpretation of reality the ultimate determiner of truth, but that is exactly what agnosticism implies. As God's explanation of the universe is deemed unnecessary, the limited vantage point of the human interpreter functions as the ultimate position of authority, whether or not this is admitted by the agnostic. And while agnostics freely admit their ignorance concerning many things, as do atheists, they nevertheless remain quite certain that God has not or cannot reveal His existence and nature to humanity. These claims also imply that reality has no necessary need of God's power for its beginning and continued existence, it bears no marks of His design and creative activity, and the limited vantage point of a finite human being is sufficient to make such statements as authoritative and true.

The agnostic's justification for making such claims will be discussed later, but note well that the scope of the agnostic's claims concern not only God, man, and reality, but also the nature of knowledge, truth, and ultimate authority, despite the agnostic's assertions to the contrary.

Concerning Morality

It follows, then, that if the agnostic's interpretation is the final arbiter of the nature of God, mankind, and reality, as well as knowledge, truth, and ultimate authority, he or she is therefore the ultimate judge of right and wrong. If we cannot know the nature of God, or even be sure of His very existence, what claim could such a God (if He exists) have upon humanity? To what higher authority can mankind look, or to what standard of morality is mankind obligated, if the existence and nature of God is unknown? In the absence of love and fear of God, the agnostic, along with the atheist, is free to do whatever seems right in his or her own eyes. Even when a god or higher being is viewed as a necessary (though imaginary) basis of morality, mankind remains the ultimate moral authority. And if no higher authority can be known, no ultimate accountability for one's actions can be known.

Again, this is not to say that all agnostics live outwardly immoral lives relative to Christians—it is just to say that the dogmatic assertion that God's existence and nature cannot be known is a claim of independence from the laws and ultimate judgment of God. The claim that God cannot be known implies no ultimate standard of right and wrong, no ultimate accountability, and no ultimate judgment.[2] Thus, the claims of the agnostic are comprehensive in their ethics as they extend to the moral government of the universe, the ultimate destination of humanity after death, and the existence of ultimate accountability in the hereafter for bad behavior in the present life. To say that the existence and nature of God cannot be known is to say a great deal.

Endnotes

[1] A favorite description of the universe and its contents used by unbelievers.

[2] This is not to deny the existence of temporal, agreed upon standards or "social contracts" by which societies govern themselves. But, apart from God, no *ultimate* standard for these "contracts" or *ultimate*

judgment of their norms exists. And while self preservation and interest play a large part in such contracts, they give clear evidence of the fact that God has written His law on every heart (Romans 2:14-15).

11

The Presumption of Omniscience

In illustrating the common assumptions underlying both agnosticism and atheism, we return to our ongoing conversation between Mr. Christian ("C") and Mr. Agnostic ("A"), who has since exchanged his profession of atheism for agnosticism.

Mr. A: Greetings, Mr. C, I have good news for you!

Mr. C: Greetings to you, Mr. A, I am anxious to hear it.

Mr. A: I am no longer an atheist and I owe it all to you!

Mr. C: I am thrilled, Mr. A. Will you be coming to our Bible study this Thursday?

Mr. A: Oh, no, Mr. C, nothing like that. Our discussions on atheism convinced me that I do not possess the omniscience necessary to declare God's nonexistence, for after all, I am only human. How could one with mental and physical limitations possibly know enough of every aspect of the universe and beyond to declare that God does not exist?

Mr. C: Excellent, Mr. A.

Mr. A: Yes, Mr. C, you have convinced me to be an agnostic.

Mr. C: A what?

Mr. A: You know, an agnostic. Your arguments were so convincing that I was forced to admit my limitations as a human being. Constrained by these limits, I cannot possibly know whether or not God exists, and it is sheer arrogance for anyone to claim such knowledge, don't you agree, Mr. C?

After all, God is so much higher than us, is He not? Did you not say so yourself?

Mr. C: Uh...

Mr. A: I was arrogant, but I have been humbled. I was unreasonable in presuming to know what I could not know, so I am now being reasonable in admitting my limitations.

Mr. C: That sounds like quite a transformation, Mr. A. Can I ask a few more questions?

Mr. A: Please do. Perhaps your erudition will convince me to be a Buddhist.

Mr. C: Humble indeed, Mr. A.

Mr. A: I jest, do ask your questions.

Mr. C: Do you claim it is *impossible* for any human to know whether or not God exists?

Mr. A: Yes.

Mr. C: Are you also saying that no human could possibly know what God is like, even if He did exist?

Mr. A: That is correct. It is reasonable that we cannot possibly know what God is like and whether or not He exists.

Mr. C: If God did exist, could He make himself known to His creatures?

Mr. A: No.

Mr. C: I thought you said we cannot know what God is like?

Mr. A: We can't.

Mr. C: So why are you now telling me what God is like?

Mr. A: I am not telling you what God is like.

Mr. C: You are telling me that either He does not exist, or if He does, He either lacks the power or wisdom to reveal Himself to His creatures, or He willingly chooses not to do so. How do you know this?

Mr. A: Because He has not revealed Himself.

Mr. C: How do you know He has not, or could not, reveal Himself?

Mr. A: I know where you are going with this, Mr. C. Okay, I am unable as a finite human being to know for sure that God *could not* reveal himself, and that he *cannot possibly* be known. I would need to possess knowledge about God to say such things, and I have already said we cannot know God. I get it, I am contradicting myself and being reasonable and unreasonable at the same time. Is that where you are going with this?

Mr. C: Correct, and then some. To claim that God can or cannot do something is to claim knowledge of God, of whom you say we cannot have knowledge—a contradiction. And what would someone need to know to legitimately claim what a transcendent God could or could not do, apart from God telling him?

Mr. A: I guess he would have to be God Himself. How else could he know everything about what God could or could not do?

Mr. C: Correct. As we discussed before, to say what God can and cannot be and what He can and cannot do, apart from His revealing it to you, is to place faith in your own opinion concerning the ultimate nature of

God and the universe. We are finite
and ill-equipped to say such things, at
least with legitimate authority. You
have again made yourself the final
authority with respect to interpreting
the nature of God and the universe,
while not possessing the ability to do
so.

Mr. A: Who said anything about the universe?

Mr. C: By saying God cannot reveal Himself,
you have essentially said that nothing
we know of the universe gives evidence
of His existence or displays anything
of His nature.

Mr. A: Okay, it does not.

Mr. C: But how do you know?

Mr. A: Because I look at the universe and
do not see any evidence for God. I
get your original point that I cannot
say God *cannot* be known, because
that is contradicting myself in saying
what God is like when I said He
cannot be known. It is making myself
like God in defining the ultimate
nature of God in what He can or

cannot be or do, even though I do not have the capacity to do so. So I am now revising my position.

Mr. C: Okay, let's hear it.

Mr. A: Maybe He does exist, maybe He doesn't, I just don't know. I won't venture to say whether or not He can be known, or what He can or cannot do, as I am in no place to do so, and I would only be contradicting myself if I did. Therefore I will say this—I just don't know.

Mr. C: Are you saying there is no evidence?

Mr. A: I know what you will say if I say there is no evidence. You will say I must be omniscient to say so, that I must know everything there is to know in the universe to say there is absolutely no evidence. So I will say this maybe there is evidence and maybe not, but I have not personally seen any evidence of God's existence, so I just don't know.

Mr. C: I see.

Mr. A: Mr. C, at least take comfort in that

you did not convince me to become a
Buddhist. But it appears that I am
still an agnostic, although a smarter
and more reasonable one, thanks to
you. Now, in all humility, I do not
know that God exists, but I do know
that the value of my house and the
hard-earned favorable opinion of my
neighbors will decline if I do not
finish the painting I started this
morning. Thank you again for your
insights, Mr. C, always a pleasure!

Mr. C: You are welcome, I think.

It appears that things did not turn out
exactly as Mr. C would have liked, though he
did expose the initial dogmatic agnosticism of
Mr. A as groundless, obliging Mr. A to revise his
view. Also, Mr. C reiterated the principles that
answered Mr. A's former atheism, a foundation
that will ultimately prove helpful in answering
Mr. A's new and improved agnosticism. We
observed that the dogmatic assertion, "God's
existence and attributes *cannot* be known,"
is based on the same flawed assumption of

atheism that presumes the finite perspective of a human being as sufficient to know that which omniscience alone can know. Moreover, Mr. A's claim that the existence and nature of God *cannot* be known is actually a claim to know what God is able or willing to do (such as make Himself known to His creatures), though Mr. A claimed that God could not be known. This, of course, is a self-defeating contradiction, a claim to know what the agnostic says cannot be known. Moreover, by assuming the ultimate authority to define what God can and cannot be and do, Mr. A placed unjustified faith in his own ability to know what he stated could not be known (and could not be known apart from a direct revelation from God). Thus, in asking agnostics how they know what they say they know, we see the unreasonable and self-contradicting faith assumptions underlying their claims. This renders worthless their best arguments, since they are built on unreasonable and false assumptions. Again, how can one who does not know what is in my garage or my antique box tell me what the transcendent God of the universe can be or do?

12

The Denial of the Obvious

I previously mentioned two types of agnosticism: One that dogmatically asserts that the nature and existence of God cannot be known (the version addressed above), and a "kinder and gentler agnosticism" that merely admits to a lack of evidence. In the most recent exchange, we watched Mr. A go from the former to the latter when confronted with the irrationality of his claim that the existence and nature of God *cannot* be known. Thus, Mr. A appears to have exchanged his dogmatic and unjustified agnosticism (that of defining what God can or cannot be or do) for an admission of his own inadequacy. He now admits that evidence of God's nature and existence might exist, though he claims never to have seen it. Has Mr. A finally become reasonable in his assertions regarding God's existence and attributes? Is his "kinder and gentler" agnosticism a reasonable form of unbelief? Does it more satisfactorily take into account the limitations of the human vantage point and knowledge? Let's listen in…

Mr. C: Good morning Mr. A, the new paint on your house looks great.

Mr. A: Thank you, Mr. C. You are a gentleman, even if you are a religious zealot. I am anxious to hear your response to my more humble and reasonable agnosticism.

Mr. C: You are too kind, Mr. A. If I understand you correctly, you now admit that evidence for God's existence might exist, but you just have not seen any, correct?

Mr. A: Correct.

Mr. C: So, it is possible that others may have

seen evidence for God's existence that you have not seen?

Mr. A: I do not think so, as we are all human with similar experiences.

Mr. C: So there may be evidence, but no one has seen it?

Mr. A: Yes.

Mr. C: If no one has access to any of the evidence, we are back to your original contention that no evidence for God exists. This could be because God cannot, has not, or will not reveal His existence. Or, if He has, He chose to not reveal it *to us*. You're back to claiming what God can or cannot be or do, which you are incapable of doing.

Mr. A: Okay, *maybe* others have seen evidence, but I have not, and I cannot be convinced until I do.

Mr. C: Scripture tells us everything in the universe, including your conscience, the stars, a baby, and the food on your table, is clear and obvious evidence.

Mr. A: But I do not see anything as evidence

for God's existence. You say it is, and I say it isn't—it's a draw. You have your opinion, I have my opinion. Who's to say who is right?

Mr. C: I see, but ultimately my interpretation is based on Scripture's testimony that all of reality bears the mark of God's wisdom, design, and power, such that all are without excuse.

Mr. A: But I do not accept Scripture as true.

Mr. C: So we can now agree that we have different foundations upon which we base our interpretation of reality. My foundation is Scripture, yours is your own opinion. The issue is not my opinion versus yours, but your opinion versus God's Word. This is an important distinction.

Mr. A: But I don't believe Scripture is God's Word.

Mr. C: So, again, you are resting your interpretation of all of reality, including your view of Scripture, on your own opinion, which we have already shown to be an inadequate foundation upon which to interpret the ultimate nature of God and reality. You can't tell me what is in my antique box, but you know for sure that Scripture is not God's Word. So you are still functioning as the ultimate authority in the universe in your interpretation of the nature of God and all of reality. By the way, how do you know Scripture is not God's Word?

Mr. A: It is full of fairy tales and myths, like Jonah in a whale. Even some of your own Christian scholars say it is full of myths.

Mr. C: Yes, some scholars appear to help you more than those of us who believe the Bible, Mr. A. Yet it appears that your interpretation of Scripture is based on the presumption that God does not exist, for if He did, miracles would be reasonable and expected. To reject the Bible because you reject miracles is to presume God does not exist or, if He did, to presume what He could or would do or not do, which you admit you cannot know. We discussed this earlier.

Mr. A: You are frustrating.

Mr. C: My apologies. I see in everything evidence for God's existence, while you see none of it. I see my understanding as reasonable, and you see your interpretation as reasonable. Correct?

Mr. A: Correct.

Mr. C: So viewing the beauty, design, and 'miracle' of the universe and seeing no evidence of God is reasonable, correct?

Mr. A: Yes.

Mr. C: Allow me to tell you a story. Brothers Jack and George went to a museum and viewed beautiful sculptures and paintings, including Rembrandts and Monets. Jack exclaimed, 'Oh the brilliance and skill of the artists!' To which George replied, 'How do you know? I see no evidence of artists, let alone great artists in these works.'

Who is reasonable, Jack or George?

Mr. A: Jack, of course.

Mr. C: The next day, while playing a sophisticated computer game, Jack exclaims, 'The programmers of this are brilliant!' To which George responds, 'Programmers? I don't see any evidence of programmers!' Who is being reasonable?

Mr. A: Jack. To deny the evidence of programmers is silly.

Mr. C: Next they take a ski trip with their wives and see footprints in the snow that read, 'Will you marry me, snuggle bunny?' Jack exclaims, 'How romantic, a marriage proposal in the snow, and such a cute nickname!' To which George responds, 'How do you know someone wrote that?' Who is more reasonable?

Mr. A: Of course, any reasonable person would know that someone wrote that in the snow.

Mr. C: Would the evidence be more compelling if there were more intelligible words or less words in the snow?

Mr. A: More words. Maybe snow falling from trees could produce a word or two (though they were footprints), but regardless, the more words and complexity of the sentences, the greater the evidence that someone wrote it.

Mr. C: So, if an entire encyclopedia entry was in the snow, it would be greater evidence than a single sentence?

Mr. A: Of course.

Mr. C: So, a finger painting could be an accident, but a Mona Lisa requires a skilled painter?

Mr. A: Exactly.

Mr. C: If you took a trip to the moon and found a working computer on the surface, what would you conclude?

Mr. A: I was not the first one there, of course.

Mr. C: Could it have just happened over time?

Mr. A: A computer, programmed and working? Of course not, that would be an unreasonable interpretation.

Mr. C: Are you aware that a blade of grass is more sophisticated than anything mankind has yet to produce in all of its technological efforts?

Mr. A: Yes, I took biology.

Mr. C: That a single butterfly is more sophisticated than an F-22 fighter jet?

Mr. A: Granted.

Mr. C: So tell me why it is unreasonable to deny that artists, programmers, or writers in the snow exist, but entirely reasonable to deny the designer and builder of an ant, a flower, a baby, billions of life forms, including trillions upon trillions of single cells, each more sophisticated than anything man has ever created? Are you more or less reasonable than George in his claim of no evidence for artists, programmers, and a potential groom? According to your own principles, would not greater sophistication and complexity be greater evidence of the genius of the designer?

Mr. A: Okay, but I don't see the evidence.

Mr. C: You have an opinion, but how is it a reasonable opinion given the evidence? You may reject my interpretation, but my interpretation is reasonable according to your own criteria of what constitutes reasonableness. When it comes to the existence and nature of God, contrary to your own principles, you go from being reasonable to exercising pure blind faith in your own opinion.

Mr. A: Why would I do that, Mr. C?

Mr. C: Scripture says we sinfully suppress the obvious truth because we are unrighteous and hostile to God.[1] The existence of artists does not have ultimate moral implications for our lives, so we easily admit their existence in the face of the evidence. But God's existence requires our sincere worship and obedience to Him, the proper response to our Creator. His existence dethrones our assumed position as captain of our own ship, as ultimate interpreter of the nature of God, man, reality, knowledge, truth, authority, and ethics. No one can approach the existence and nature of God with the neutral objectivity of approaching a painting in a museum. People who like to call their own shots have a compelling (though unreasonable) interest in denying God. Would this not account for the fact that they lay aside their usual reasonableness and question God's existence in spite of the clear, conspicuous, comprehensive, and compelling evidence to the contrary?

Mr. A: So, are you saying I am willfully denying the obvious because I desire my own way and refuse to worship God?

Mr. C: Yes, and that is the same reason why people deny the Bible is God's Word. The evidence that the Bible is God's Word is just as clear, conspicuous, comprehensive, and compelling as the evidence that God created everything in the universe, but people willfully reject it.[2] Those who view the clear fingerprints of God in the beauty and order of the universe and deny God as the Creator will always deny the beauty and excellence of the Gospel of Jesus Christ and the Bible as God's written revelation.

Mr. A: So you are saying I am not neutral and objective in interpreting the evidence, that I have an ax to grind?

Mr. C: Yes. Mr. A, do you know why Christ said, 'He who is not with me is against Me'?[3]

Mr. A: No, why?

Mr. C: Because He is God in the flesh, and you cannot be neutral to the One who created you, gives you all good things, to whom you owe all love, honor, and obedience. We are all created by God to enjoy Him and give Him glory. To be 'neutral' is to suppress the clear knowledge of God in sinful ingratitude, to reject His purpose and treat Him with contempt. Sometimes to ignore someone is greater hatred than active opposition. 'Neutrality' toward God is contempt for the moral obligation to love, honor, and obey one's Creator. No middle ground exists for people created by Him.

Mr. A: My garden needs watering, so I must go utilize the wisdom bestowed on me by, well, who knows?

Mr. C: Well, I leave you to 'who knows.' I will go thank God and my wife for the steak that will be waiting for me when I get home. God richly provides for His creatures, just as He provides for you and gave you wisdom to care for your garden. Indeed, 'He did not leave Himself without witness, in that He did good and gave you rains from heaven and fruitful seasons, satisfying your hearts with food and gladness.'[4] Indeed, He has provided for you a Savior to deliver you from the penalty for your willful sin of ingratitude.

Mr. A: Please tell me more…

Mr. C: In John 3:16 it says…

Mr. A: Just kidding! I best be going, my

wife's marvelous stuffed jalapeños beckon me. They are so good I sneak a second helping before I go to bed, but don't tell my wife, she thinks they give me nightmares. Anyway, I need to get to sleep at a decent hour so I can get up early to pull weeds.

Mr. C: [Sigh] You should have good weather for it, Mr. A, the beautiful red and orange sunset foretells a nice day for you. Perhaps I'll see you tomorrow; I have to trim some trees with my new chain saw.

Mr. A: I look forward to seeing you in the morning! Perhaps I'll give some more thought to what you have said.

Mr. C: Sweet dreams, Mr. A.

Having "progressed" from his more strident agnosticism that claims God *cannot* be known, Mr. A took refuge in the "kinder and gentler" agnosticism that merely claims a lack of evidence. In making the switch, however, Mr. A did not change his unreasonable blind faith in his own opinion concerning the ultimate nature of God and the universe, but only changed its facade. To claim no evidence is to assume knowledge of the entire universe and assert that either God does not exist, or, if He does, He cannot or will not make His existence and attributes known. But to make such a claim, one would have to know of the existence and attributes of the God that cannot be known. To allow for the possibility of evidence, but deny access to such evidence, is little different from claiming no evidence. In either case, all of the "miraculous" beauty and design of the universe is interpreted by Mr. A as bearing no evidence of God.

This very claim is *contrary to the agnostic's own principles*. It unjustifiably assumes that a finite human being is capable of having the necessary knowledge to make such an interpretation as authoritative and true. The agnostic readily admits to the artist behind great art, the programmer behind the computer program, and the writer behind the proposal in the snow, all the while affirming that greater design and complexity give greater evidence of a designer. At the same time, the agnostic claims that the greatest design and complexity give no evidence, contrary to his own principles. Why does the normally reasonable and logical agnostic become so unreasonable and illogical with respect to the existence and nature of God? Because to admit God exists is to admit one's own responsibility to thank, worship, and obey God as creator and provider, to admit liability to judgment for not doing so, and to deny one's own presumed authority and independence. To admit that the Bible is God's Word is to do the same. And so it is that no one approaches the issue of God's existence and attributes with a detached objectivity, and so it is why a normally reasonable person will go to such great lengths to deny the obvious. To borrow a quote from Irving Kristol, "When we lack the will to see things as they really are, there is nothing so mysterious as the obvious."

Endnotes

[1] See Romans 1:18-21, John 3:19-20.

[2] Unbelievers sinfully suppress and reject both general and special revelation. See Luke 16:31; John 1:9-14; 5:36-40, 46-47; 8:34-47; 10:1-16; 1 Corinthians 1:18-24; 2:6-16; 2 Peter 1:20-21.

[3] Matthew 12:30.

[4] Acts 14:17.

13

A Reality Check

The exchanges between Mr. C and Mr. A are designed to illustrate certain principles and techniques of apologetics, and should not be viewed as typical discussions between a believer and unbeliever. To the contrary, the dialogue includes a fair amount of exaggeration in that it went as long and far as it did, as cordially as it did, and in the amount of ground Mr. A was willing to concede to Mr. C. Most Christians have experienced the difficulty of disabusing unbelievers of their notions of God and the universe, and realize there is no way to predict how a given conversation will go and end. Unbelievers will concede a great deal regarding non-essentials. But when they sense that their ultimate object of faith, their most deeply held assumptions or presuppositions about God and reality are about to be exposed as the unreasonable sin that they are, they will change the subject, quit the discussion, call you names, ignore you, persecute you, or otherwise avoid the exposure of their sinful assumptions and hostility toward the God of the Bible. While many issues concerning God and the universe are fair game for discussion, the unbelievers' ultimate object of their deepest-held faith, the central and most important issue of their belief system, is strictly off limits. Indeed, apart from the work of the Holy Spirit, any true presentation of the Gospel, including a call to repent from unreasonable and idolatrous faith to faith in Christ alone, will always be strenuously resisted and rejected. The power of God alone can bring someone to true faith in Christ. Nonetheless, we are called to proclaim and defend the Gospel to unbelievers, leaving the results to God.

14

Summary

We have seen that the critique of agnosticism closely resembles that of atheism, for contrary to the view that agnosticism corrects the inherent problems of atheism, the faith assumptions upon which atheists and agnostics make their arguments are virtually identical. In fact, the same assumptions underlie all unbelieving arguments against the God of Scripture. Thus, by understanding the unreasonable blind faith underlying atheism and agnosticism, the reader will be better able to identify and expose the faith assumptions behind all unbelieving arguments.

Like the claims of the atheist, the agnostic's claims that "the existence of God *cannot* be known," or "the evidence for His existence is lacking," are actually sweeping assertions about the ultimate nature of God, man, reality, knowledge, truth, authority, and ethics. In highlighting the sweeping scope of these claims, we observed how ill-equipped the agnostic is to make them.

In examining the authority to make claims about the ultimate nature of God and the universe, we asked the simple question, "How do you know what you say you know?" Like atheism, agnosticism rests on faith in unwarranted human opinion. We again saw that a finite being, constrained by five senses, three dimensions, and seventy or so years on earth, is not equipped to make dogmatic, comprehensive, and trustworthy statements about the ultimate origin and nature of God and the universe. Without revelation from the God that "cannot be known," or for whom the "evidence is lacking," agnostics are as ill equipped as atheists to make dogmatic assertions about God and the universe.

Lastly, we noted that a "kinder and gentler" agnosticism that alleges a *lack of evidence* to either affirm or deny God's existence operates on the same faith assumptions of the more dogmatic variety. Also, an appeal to "a lack of evidence" is contrary to the agnostic's own principles of interpretation and knowledge. Reason quickly becomes unreasonable in the face of the profound implications of God's existence and authority over the unbeliever's life. In defense of their assumed independence, Scripture tells us the agnostic and all unbelievers

> suppress the truth in unrighteousness, because that which is known about God is evident within them; for God made it evident to them. For since the creation of the world His invisible attributes, His eternal power and divine nature, have been clearly seen, being understood through what has been made, so that they are without excuse. For even though they knew God, they did not honor Him as God or give thanks, but they became futile in their speculations, and their foolish heart was darkened.[1]

And so it is that the agnostic and atheist deny the obvious. Unwilling to relinquish their assumed place of authority and independence to acknowledge their complete dependence upon their Creator, they define Him into obscurity or out of existence.

Endnotes

[1]   Romans 1:18b-21.

CONCLUDING REMARKS

15

A Proper Approach

We have but briefly touched on a small sample of arguments against the existence of the God of Scripture, yet have examined a basis for understanding the nature of all such arguments, providing a framework for effectively responding to those who would undermine our faith in Christ. And like all biblical principles, proper application takes study, reflection, experience, and time.

Also, no formula exists that should be exclusively applied to produce predictable results, for salvation is by the Spirit of God and the Word of God only.[1] Neither a proper apologetic method nor a proper evangelistic method guarantees the unbeliever will acknowledge the unreasonableness of unbelief, nor respond in saving faith. The sinner is hostile to the God of Scripture and is neither neutral nor objective in viewing arguments for faith in Christ and against unbelief. The power of God alone can change the sinful heart.

Accordingly, as Francis Schaeffer so ably counseled us, even while the ultimate issues of the Gospel remain the same for anyone, people have different personalities and should be treated as important and unique, created by God in His image. When we apply rules mechanically or indiscriminately, we neglect to honor people as individuals.[2] Love, wisdom, and ears for listening must always guide our interactions with unbelievers. Truth is unchanging, but it must always be applied with love and care.

Moreover, the life of Christ in the believer presents perhaps the greatest apologetic argument for Christianity. The sacrificial love of Christ is a powerful message, with or without words, while a lack of love renders any apologetic approach fruitless: "If I have *the gift of* prophecy, and know all mysteries and all knowledge; and if I have all faith, so as to remove mountains, but do not have love, I am nothing" (1 Corinthians 13:2). Anyone can win an argument, but patience and love toward our antagonists presents a far greater challenge, often producing far greater results. None of this should be interpreted, however, as advocating love over and against truth, for love without truth is equally futile.

And whatever approach one takes in defending and proclaiming the Gospel to unbelievers, the method and message must supremely honor Christ as creator, redeemer, and Lord, and be true to what Scripture has revealed to us about the nature of God, mankind, all of created reality, and Scripture itself. Apologetic methods that compromise the authority and historical accuracy of Scripture, or attempt to make Scripture compatible with the unbelieving worldview, dishonor God and harm the faith of believers, while affirming the faith assumptions of unbelief. We are called to be faithful in living, proclaiming, and defending Christ and the Gospel.

Endnotes

[1] I personally have seen the most fruit in my dialogues with unbelievers when I have said little and merely pointed to passages of Scripture for the unbeliever to read.

[2] See Francis A. Schaeffer, *The God Who Is There* in *Francis A. Schaeffer Trilogy* (Wheaton: Crossway, 1990; Originally published by InterVarsity Press, 1968), 130-31.

16

Apologetics and the Gospel

The call to faith in Christ is a call to repent of misplaced faith in the idols of our own making, for such was central to Christ's preaching ministry: "Repent and believe in the gospel" (Mark 1:15). Repentance is from sin, and what greater sin than idolatry—and what greater idol than our own explanation of God and reality, a god of our own making?[1] Such was at the heart of Adam's sin in the garden when he assumed his own interpretation was authoritative in choosing between obeying or disobeying the word of God. Such *presumed* independence from the authority of God is at the heart of every sin. We are warned that "he who trusts in his own heart is a fool" (Proverbs 28:26). This apologetic method says exactly that.

In exposing the unbelievers' unwarranted and unreasonable faith in their own opinion, we expose their faith in a false "god" of their making, which they must repent to embrace Christ. We proclaim the Gospel in our defense of it, and we do so in faithfulness to Christ with grace and love toward the unbeliever.

Of course, God and Scripture need no defense, nor does God need us to bring His Gospel message—He is infinitely capable of accomplishing His perfect will apart from our efforts. Yet, He has called us to the honor of participating in His eternal purposes and has ordained the defense and proclamation of the Gospel message to that end.

Thus, a primary goal of apologetics is bringing people to the lifesaving message of salvation through faith in the perfect person and saving work of Christ alone. As God appointed Scripture as the sufficient means of the Holy Spirit to convict unbelievers of sin and bring them to repentance and salvation, so the ultimate purpose of any apologetic encounter is to bring the unbeliever face-to-face with the Gospel of Christ in Scripture, including what Scripture says about unbelief.

And as we learn to apply biblical apologetic principles in our contact with unbelievers, by God's grace, our faith and ability to respond to irrational unbelieving arguments with love and grace will be improved. When our starting point in all things is the nature of our glorious Triune God who created, ordered, and upholds all things, whose glory is displayed in all of creation, we are better equipped to live in His world and interact with those who would deny the obvious. Hopefully, we will be more attentive in our conversations with unbelievers out of a genuine concern for their well-being as we graciously ask them how they know what they claim to know. And in all this, we need not be unsettled by the "learned" arguments opposing faith in Christ. May application of the principles presented here be a means to a more gracious and patient sharing of Christ as we face challenges to our faith in Him.

_____

Endnotes

[1]   See Psalm 135:15-18; Isaiah 42:17, 44:9-20.

17

A Word to Atheists and Agnostics

Finally, if you are an atheist or agnostic reading this, please know that the intent of this booklet is to bolster the faith of those who may have been hurt or intimidated by attacks against their hope and joy. We wish you no ill and would welcome the joy of embracing you as a brother or sister in Christ, to spend eternity with you in joyful fellowship with our Creator and Redeemer. Nonetheless, the words of Christ stand as a sober caution: "Whoever causes one of these little ones who believe in Me to stumble, it is better for him that a heavy millstone be hung around his neck, and that he be drowned in the depth of the sea" (Matthew 18:6). Our desire is that you not suffer the fate of those who cause the faith of God's "little ones" to stumble.

We have all sinned and fallen short of the perfect love, honor, and obedience we owe to God. We have all mocked and insulted the One who created and sustains us with good things. Yet, as our substitute, acting in our place, Christ fully satisfied the perfect righteousness required for eternal life and paid the infinite penalty demanded by our rebellion and insults against God. Through faith in Christ alone, in the acknowledgement of our sin and trust in His saving life and death alone, Christ's perfect righteousness is credited to us. United to Christ by faith, the righteousness earned by Christ's perfect life and payment of the infinite penalty for sin becomes the possession of the believer: "For the wages of sin is death, but the free gift of God is eternal life in Christ Jesus our Lord" (Romans 6:23).

For God so loved the world, that He gave His only begotten Son, that whoever believes in Him should not perish, but have eternal life. For God did not send the Son into the world to judge the world, but that the world should be saved through Him. He who believes in Him is not judged; he who does not believe has been judged already, because he has not believed in the name of the only begotten Son of God (John 3:16-18).

Christ paid an infinite price to satisfy an infinite debt, to purchase infinite glory and happiness for the infinitely unworthy. Yet, for this He is mocked, despised, and traded for that which can neither satisfy our soul nor deliver us from the penalty for sin. His warning is stark:

For what does it profit a man to gain the whole world, and forfeit his soul? For what shall a man give in exchange for his soul? For whoever is ashamed of Me and My words in this adulterous and sinful generation, the Son of Man will also be ashamed of him when He comes in the glory of His Father with the holy angels (Mark 8:36-38).

Christ bids you, "Come to Me, all who are weary and heavy-laden, and I will give you rest" (Matthew 11:28). From a heart of infinite love, He offers you an infinite gift of grace.

We wish you the greatest blessings of God as found through faith in Christ alone, in whom is infinite merit and forgiveness for the worst of sinners. Our hope and prayer is that we may stand together with you in God's presence, blameless and with great joy.[1]

Endnotes

[1]   See Jude 24

Acknowledgments

The many friends and colleagues who took the time to read and comment on this little book have been a great blessing. I would particularly like to thank William Edgar, David McWilliams, James White, Eric Arnall, Dustyn Eudaly, Steve Webb, and W. K. Miley for their thoughtful critiques and insights. The principles presented here are largely drawn from Cornelius Van Til's application of biblical truth to the theological discipline of apologetics. And while the volume and complexity of his work pose a challenge to any who would read, understand, and simplify his method, I have been greatly assisted in the task by the excellent scholarship of K. Scott Oliphint, John Frame, and the late Greg Bahnsen. To God be all the glory.

About the Author

Craig and his wife Angelica live and minister in Pennsylvania, where they are delighted to be redeemed in Christ. Craig received his AB in Economics from Cal Berkeley, MBA from UCLA Anderson School of Management, ThM from Dallas Theological Seminary, and PhD in Systematic Theology from Westminster Theological Seminary. He is the author of *The Infinite Merit of Christ: The Glory of Christ's Obedience in the Theology of Jonathan Edwards*; *Reading Religious Affections: A Study Guide to Jonathan Edwards' Classic on the Nature of True Christianity*; and *God the Reason: How Infinite Excellence Gives Unbreakable Faith*. Craig's blog can be found at www.pilgrimsrock.com.

Unbreakable Faith Course

The Box and *God the Reason* are part of an enjoyable and faith-building video course for adults and mature teenagers called *Unbreakable Faith*. With colorful slides and illustrations, *Unbreakable Faith:*

✓ exalts the infinite excellence of God's perfections
✓ nurtures a deeper love for God
✓ strengthens joy, faith and assurance in Christ and Scripture
✓ immunizes believers against the most sophisticated arguments of unbelief
✓ gives simple and effective ways to address the deepest theological difficulties and mysteries

The course can also be taken for home school credit in a fully self-contained online format, including all exams. For more information and sample videos visit www.pilgrimsrock.com.

CRAIG BIEHL

GOD
THE REASON

GOD
THE REASON
How Infinite Excellence
Gives Unbreakable Faith

BIEHL

"God the Reason, is a remarkable work. It presents theology proper—the knowledge of God—in all of its transcendent importance and breadth. It does so in a way that is accessible, clear and spiritually invigorating. If you are thirsting for a deeper and more personal knowledge of the Lord of the universe, drink deeply of this study. The divine perfections celebrated here will bless your life, stir your reason and ground your faith on an unmovable foundation."

—Dr. Peter A. Lillback, President, Westminster Theological Seminary

Carpenter's Son Publishing